TAPLASH MEDITATIONS

by

Napier Marten

A limited edition of which this is number 95 of 250.

i

TAPLASH MEDITATIONS by Napier Marten

Published by Mirthquake
Mirthquake is a registered trademark.

Illustrations by Johnny Bull
johnny@johnnybull.uk

Typesetting by Simon Crook
linearfoxgraphics@gmail.com

Printed in Wales by Gomer Press

FOREWORD

"You can tear a poem apart to see what makes it technically tick" said Dylan Thomas, and in the end, you are left "with the mystery of being moved by the words."

Thomas fell in love with language as a child, cherishing its sounds and intimations; a similar enthusiasm for words, some rare, some commonplace, is present throughout Napier Marten's collection 'Taplash Meditations.'

What makes these poems such a rewarding read is they are grounded in a strong sense of place. Deeply felt and known landscapes and settings abound from the loving simplicity of 'A Cabin in Connecticut' to 'The Galway Hooker' fishing for herring in rough seas off Donegal, to blue corn tortillas, bougainvillea and hibiscus to be found amidst the mystical cloudscapes of the sierras of Jalisco and Morelos in Mexico.

Above all there are a series of richly atmospheric portraits of the land, sea, sky and seasons of Findhorn, Morayshire and Nairnshire in Northeast Scotland. Places of great beauty and harshness where "weathered men with weathered hands" talk "of fuel, of crude, of feed and food" while the scent of DERV catches in their throats at a Ploughing Match one late autumn afternoon. The deliberate use and repetition of hard, practical words like adze, chisel, dowel and chamfer, further anchor the poems in a closely realised world of work while the "holes and gaps" as Thomas described them, allow the readers imagination to fly above the stark beauty of the highland rivers and moors, and engage in the kind of meditative reflections that give the compilation its title.

Jamie Reid June 2024

My sincere thanks to these dear friends and family for their encouragement, support and suggestions:

Elva Corrie, Jude Spiro, Peter Brightman, Sarah MacInnes, Amabel Clarke, Aidan Dun, Ruth Aymer Marten, Simon Crook, Mark Jackson, Norrie Maclaren, The Is It Strong? Club, Annie Fowler, and Christabel Hunter.

A particular thank you to Johnny Bull for his fabulous illustrations.

CONTENTS

INTRODUCTION

I am deeply grateful to those who gently and without relent, twisted my arm to complete this compilation of poems. For a long time, I desired to write and likewise procrastinated until, in late 2017, I was given a few pointers about how to get pen on paper. When time and tide of inner perceptions coalesced, I did so. Landscapes and seascapes express themselves to us and have the capacity to move us, even to tears. I endeavour to express my experience of this in writing. These poems are notes really, annotated in the brief instances of these conversations I have been fortunate to experience.

Napier Marten, June 2024

THIS RUSTY NAIL DAWN

A Cabin In Connecticut

In this house is strong Medicine,
Clapperboard and creaking,
Tree girt oasis, small, in sky blue,
Crow guarded, buzzard-eyed and chipmunk.

Winter fog wraps all outby.
Within, sun shines in every room
By her hand of knowing gentleness,
Caressing our eyes, touching our hearts.

Ancestors are with us,
Living simply like us.
We eat, we sleep, we laugh,
Learning wider and deeper as we open.

Crystal, rock, lantern,
Turkey wing, pouch and beads.
Wristed selfless turquoise,
Wampum belts and headdress.

We are enriched, blessed and beautiful,
Softened beyond knowing.
Under strict instructions to be us,
To be of Love and duty free.

East River Road, Connecticut

An Ogham Stone In Wicklow

She was spoken of,
I say 'she' for that was the understanding,
In hushed reverence.
Touchstone to long-lost past,
Gravid myth, legend, falsehoods.

How long shall we traipse?
Is she solo?
Are there cohorts, consorts?
Long lost relatives of
This grid of earthly energy,
Lodged by ancient understanding,
Delicious, complex simplicity
To ancient, once connected times.

In the middle of a green somewhere
Crotchety tumbledown gate,
Striking across the mire,
Grass and sedge,
In the distance a darkened glade.

Taken by surprise,
Brilliant shards of sunlight pierced the urman thicket
Where she stood, recondite, mysterious,
To guide we weary trekkers.

Vile rusty barbed-wire fence,
Trouser rip, blood and curse,
Ground grew boggier
Squelching steps in flatulent abandon.

A flash of Sylvan scene b'rayed
Our vessel, magic artefact,
Stowaway in a somnolent landscape.

Bring gnosis to we who visit.

Portal to the present from far ago.
She stands singular,
Twice fathom high,
Worked and honed by long forgotten fingers
In long forgotten ceremonies.

Along one side,
Gently rubbed by centuries of wind and rain
Were carved at different angles,
Lines.

A language to be guessed by God or
Sheer doggedness,
Exuding her dominion with clear intent.
We mollify,
Subdued in the presence of inanimate life.

A Memory Of Wicklow, Eire

Crestone

Across a small divide,
Our flowering meadows met.
You the colour of honey-gatherers,
Your tumbling locks the mountain's
Ridges, cwms and cories of the
Rainbow dwelling Wise Ones' places.

A fortunate bird, still pre-rigour warm,
Found your soft hand's clasped embrace
Bidding fond farewell beneath trees,
In prayer, grace, gratitude for Creation.

No reproach from ravens' sighing wings,
Nor gliding vultures' fingertips.
Gazing across the lost seabed,
Where cetacean ancestors celebrated
For the Love of it all,
Wet, warm, engaging in each other,
Their forms passed down
In rocks for our remembering,
Backed by one-time jagged snow tipped islands,
Still murmuring low tidal swishing
Bringing news of pasts and futures
Well beyond the stars.

Your delphic play
Came from the foot of day,
When I heard your crystal voice-
To the heel of the day
In dusking, bruised and bruising peaks
...and portals.
We left under the darkening brow
Of a sinking sun,
Deepening heart of the departing day.

Crestone, Colorado

7

Dogs

Dogs -
Trust your noses
Trust your tails.

I know Alfie, Lester, Douglas,
You know Jess, Munro, Buddy.

Enthusiasts all, unbowed, uncowed.
We love you.

Charlie kept his marbles well beyond his years,
Bad hips mind.

Slobber-dobber faces, pink tongues lolling,
On the beach, ten miles for you, one for us.
We understand your instant gratifications.

Hell, WILL YOU LISTEN,
Shouting with the whistle,
You are oblivious.

Perry's got a tick.

Ever patient Mungo's rolled in corruption,
Then licks himself.

Jackson brought his toy.

You are individuals,
Cleo, Squeak, Harley.

Boaz ate the whole cake and was very ill.
Gums, Old Man was a grinner.

Beings of another realm in ours,
Lucy, Longbow, ever farting Rolph.

No failsooths you, nor guileless lovers,
Without complaint, without opinion.

Should we, in friendship, be so different?

Findhorn, Morayshire

9

Jeff The Angelic Postman

Jeff the Angelic Postman loved Gus,
And of course, the other way around.
When church at Christmas was lovely,
Jeff gazed deeply into the centre of Man,
On his round.

Jeff the Angelic Postman, one word
Salves bruised hearts like
Witch's chickweed, cleavers and moss,
Easing the scars of agèd memories,
On his round.

Jeff the Angelic Postman will come
To Tessa's AND Alice's weddings,
For he feeds us calm and balm
With a star in his eyes,
On his round.

Jeff the Angelic Postman has had
A few days off, noticed by his friends
Who thirst for Jeff's soft hand of
Concord for all beings, offered
On his round.

Jeff the Angelic Postman lives on
An ancient seabed, risen from the deep
Too long ago, when in that time the Whale
With the Universe in her eye, saw Jeff
On his round.

Longmont, Colorado

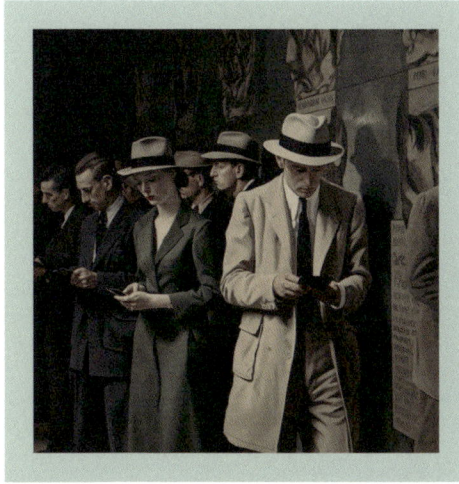

New Jersey Transit

The Terminal is trash and tribulation,
Concrete concourse, faceless faces,
Focussed one step ahead, screen fixed
In diverted somewhere, dream crushed,
Stomping, lost in unobtainable.

I reach out with hand and heart,
Extending into the
Quag slough of must be getting there,
My gesture returned with silent words
Denying all is well, truly well.

Enforced unreality of tits and arse and sugar,
Beguiles me false assurances of wealth,
Of health, ill-sought happiness on billboards, and
Serried ranks of sameness, seared meat and waffles.

Sitting brings relief.
Watching in brief respite,
Where above the tunnels lie
Perpetual stop, start, honking, spit fuelled insults.
Underneath, conveyors of conveyors,
Identikit and 'out of my way'
Mooching cops and hobos.

"Move on please"

Constant chewing, darting looks, shuffling
Observing artless oceans of rules,
B' decking every wall and stopping place,

"Move on please".

The clanging locomotive, hauling into track 21J,
Is very pleased with itself,
Tough exterior and ugliness, all angles and butch,
Shattering noise, reeking of power.

Then –

'The Gift of Possibility for Christmas' the frozen hoarding shouts.

Such trickery cloaking and shading my mind,
I would lief desire the litter strewn scalpings,
Sleepers, embankments,
Barren human choking debris of my emerging journey,
Birthing through this rusty nail dawn,
Than this morass of mortality.

Until-

Within this miresome fen,
A sweet, muted moment -
I catch the glimmer eyes of a
Hooded man across the tracks,
A spontaneous fleeting scintillation,
A smile between two brothers,
Suddenly all is well, truly well.

Secaucus, NY, NY

Remember

For Ruth & Max

Fleeting will be this briefest day,
As brief as birth, life and the end -
Till you part.

How apt, in this house of ancestors,
You turn to face the world,
Side by side,
Hand in hand,
Step in step.

Remember this day.

I see you Max, with watery eyes of your deepest affection,
And because I know you,
Full flushed in your wholesome, rightful pride of love,
For she hath seen your worth -
And you Ruth, softly glowing in golden joy,
Your love as strong as death,
He sees your profound humanity,
And I have heard your laughter ring out
As bells in everlasting peel -

Remember this day.

Let it rain,
May Champagne be flat,
The cake collapse,
A bride's maid faint,
The ring be lost,
For all is naught, bathed in your light.
It is but hilarity,
There is no diversion -

On this remembered day.
(contd.)

13

Now you are transformed,
From two into one.
And when you gaze into your children's
Violet new-born eyes -

Remember this day.

When ravens peck at the eyes of times of woe,
Of small wrongs and peccadillos scratching and fermenting,
As they will,
While I be silenced by my love for you -

Remember this day as if 't were yesterday.

Upon the marriage of Max and Ruth, Amatlan, Morelos

Self Portrait

In the mirror, only one of me I see,
My inner eye sees all of me.

September sun sets to the horizon
Indigo to apricot –

I too am in my autumn,
Bearing ripened fruit of my life
For anyone to pick,
Comforted by leaves falling through mists of memories.

My body wanes, wending its sure course,
The inner me is waxing.

Without a whit of knowing,
I trudged the purple road.
And am glad of it.

Once too quick to dismiss,
Too curious to be still.

There is more -

Gales of my early winter are brewing
Over distant ocean swells.

I must bend and flow.
(contd.)

My within extends
Above the beyond.

I am big, nimbler than they ever thought,
A trait I keep for my hands,
Square as they are, yet deft.

I have been deceitful, dishonest
Easily lead astray.
For once being so,
I pray no longer thus.

She is unique upon the Earth who is without fear.
I hear her speak oft these soft words to me.

Fate, fortune and chance are empty vessels.

Design, predetermined, protected
These my contracts.

Apricot to violet,
The chimney stack has gone from sight.

Hard frosts of my winter approach,
I am prepared,
For I have witnessed the compassion of pain.

Let oblivion be a friend,
I have seen my Light
And seen my Love.

Oakleigh, Wiltshire

The Egret And The Pepper Trees

Master of Ceremonies, puckish,
Dangerous, secret flagon by his knee,
Is in command.
Around softly roiling pots of dinner,
Pleased how we have lived and loved,
Stories be they good or ill to make us weep.

I am in the mountains' evening settled mists,
Puffs of rusty dust about my steps,
Ants on tabletops, legs and arms,
Butterflies and coffee bushes.
(contd.)

Our bums stick to wide-grouted, red, unrepentant tiles.
With constant rice wine thimbles,
Come mirthful warnings of
Missed steps, lurching flower beds, home to bed -
Blushed, flushed from long held double handed handshakes
Of welcome and farewell.

I am in the cows' complaining at the field's gate,
Demanding release to the barn and daily fresh cut grass.
I am in the air 'tween here and Da Lat Gap,
As clouds make mountains of mountains on that far horizon.

Today there were, as every day,
Midday breezes conceived on hills
By Sun and Earth's deep embrace,
Peppercorns, avocados,
Just picked shiny limes in netting bags for market,
When together we gazed across many decades chasm
As if they were not there.

I am in our memories and reminiscences of a 'back home'
We once knew, now wrapped in winter's grip.
I am in the clicking, creaking bamboo staves,
Lazy dogs, turkeys in the compound,
Tumbling puppies, so small by the one byre'd cow's hooves.

Master of Ceremonies strikes again, knowingly,
When in comes Nam Hai[1],
He who demands we finger-tip to finger-tip,
Bowed headed namaste,
Reverence for
Grandfather,
Ancestor.
These are men late of coastal means,
And Nam Hai knows them.

---

[1] *The whale, also called the Southern Sea*

18

I am in the pepper trees and saplings,
Where an egret took flight from sun's shelter,
My gentle companion's long fingers
Express his Love across the land,
Sometime overwhelmed with gratitude for his happy lot -
Deserved.

His constant love, and ever-present helpmeets,
Who, always come what may,
To which we raise then drink another thimble.

To you dear rubicund Master of Ceremonies,
Would that we were younger to know what we know now,
In setting sun, cows now with their hard fought,
Longed for scented hay.

I am in the long-gone soughing pines,
Once were monkey, snake and elephant,
In these most eastern Himalaya foothills,
Finally, I touch the soft face of Vietnam.

On staying with a long since seen friend for Tet, DaLat, Vietnam

The Forester

Dearest John,

You hung me by my belt when I was six and naughty.
Reside peacefully, where must we all in time.
Dorset burr, keenest eye for trees,
Thickened hands from years gripping gnarl and bark.
You had a twinkle.

Zephyrs in the pines moaned hushed requiems as you passed.

Galle, Sri Lanka, for the demise of a dear friend (50 words)

The Galway Hooker

Blessèd are hands with adze and chisel,
Delicate, dovetail, chamfer and dowel.
Shaving by shaving to shape a
Jaunty, boyish bluff bow,
To face chop and trough from
Connemara to Kinvarra.
Shaved to leave a soft wake from your girlish,
Sleek, sloping transom,
Flirting with the settled main.
Described of sharp, clean entry,
Red canvas aloft, sealed with pitch,
This beamish boat
With plump tumblehome,
Takes hefted herring
In pickling brine to feed the hungry.

Remembering Donegal 1993, Banchor, Nairnshire

Whale

From epochs before memory
De profundis
Came a voice above voices –

Whale.

She speaks soft words to Creation
Of Oneness binding
This Universe beyond bound.
She is unique in life without fear.
Speak too in soft words
That we may take heed.
When we do
All shall be well.

Tepoztlan, Morelos (50 words)

Winter's Evening On The Streets

(Manhattan-in-the-Marsh)

The Apple's streets are paved with gum,
Salt, jutting slabs, grates:
No prisoners taken.
In beaten slush speak tyres
Slicker-slacker, slicker-slacker
Sticky whisperings.

Walking over clacking cellar doors on Madison
In darkening hurry-to-home, holding hands,
I wear the cold, a hibernal beard, skin-pinching.

There's plenty mink on Madison,
B' jeweled, gaudy where, below
Bright chocolate-filled window sits a dosser,
Shaking, pleading, benighted, shaking,
Lost in the motion of passing-by
To sleet, to snow, to rain, to snow again.
(contd.)

Shoulder-charging, elbow-barging
With beats of holiday crescendo
Schmaltz, Nativity guilt
Here beneath the Underneath
The Underclass in steaming venting subway
Sit in tune to ills behind our masks:
Daily solitude, sore, sad hearts.
Yet stirring, always stirring,
The undead of the Apple's night
Hum and groan
To beats of living, moving, being.

Taken from my reverie,
Constant siren siren's glissando:
Caterwauling firetrucks,
Trombone-accompanied
As cops whoop-whoop like mechanical gibbons
In forests of the urban jungle.
Ambulances blare 'em scare 'em
With urgent meter's ticking even if the content isn't.

There are multitudes of missions made for each day,
Here live falsehoods that each action is history in making.
Food, food, café, food, nails, laundry, coffee, baubles,
Nails, booze, baubles, food, booze, drugs,
Block by block unchanging vanity.
Buildings for trees, snow blunting bludgeoning edges,
Branchless, leafless ever rising,
Hotchpotch hive existence,
Termites gouging out a tiny living, ants a' rush
In elevator, cab, subway:
A nature of its kind
Each step from box to box, space invading,
Every doorway a one-off meeting.

Still, it snows, dampens, and dulls.

When Great Outdoors comes to Manhattan,
Sweet piney spice of Christmas spruce
Stacked along the sidewalks,
Murmur of forests, known for lifetimes.
Have a great day, have a great afternoon
Have a great rest of the day,
Have a grate evening.
Madam, I have other plans, thank you.
All points made with pointing,
Hi guys, this is just our way to rub along.
It seems to work, offence is given, none is taken.

"I'm well wrapped" as he moves away from the door.
Is that cinnamon or cinnamon flavoured cinnamon?
Here's the canine 'Good Citizen' or so the badge displays,
For friends are more than money.
The diamond-matted paws drip as
Every dog gets greeted with an 'Awww'
From passing children,
For dogs make children of us all.

East Side, NY, NY

25

RAGE & CHOCOLATE

Ard-Daraich

Where Cairngorm and West Highlands meet,
As if under orders, rain begins.
Laggan's low waterline needs the melt
From snow shrouded Bens,
Infamous Glen Coe,
Where such bloody treachery still rankles
In long, bitter familial memories
As tidal Linnhe, rarely a mirror,
Feeds my now fêted eye,
Doubling life's joy.

Ard-Daraich, Ardnamurchan (50 words)

Ceum To Either Side

The Bin of Cullen lies low on the Firth,
Cormorants beneath its heights
Skimming to right, skimming to left
Business unknown, missions vital
Whisping wing tip vortex
Ripples
Like a minnow's rise to a fly.

In gentle breath across the waters
A lynch gate taps tuneless knockings
Against its stay.
Tide receding,
Nairn, even to Buckie
Peer through sweeping rains.

Oystercatchers'
Weeps greet sheep
Advancing linear, in nubiform peace
Grazing laver
Making sweet-salting meat.
Seals, wide-eyed, sleek and shiny.
Imagine their wet softness!
Hung above,
Quieting fog holds the Firth.

A sloping quay-
Who once came to these metal-braced granite setts?
Agin' the Revenue, brandy, tea, tobacco, spices, whisky.
Muskets for Redcoat,
Claymores for Jacobite,
Herring, fresh run salmon.

The lynch gate taps more urgent
Swaying in the rising squall,
Green paint staining
Lichen splatted stones.

Descends the misted veil,
Close horizons to shrouds,
Abstruse, mystical, obscured.
Innermost, private, solitary, mine.

Balintore, Ross & Cromarty

Coming To Ard-Tornish

Hushed whispers in the trees,
Softer than breath at my finish,
These few lasting denizens
Of ancient Caledon exhale
Still, soothing filigrees of smoke
From hidden fires of mist.

Wide the tidal river's mirror,
Slow, sure, strong,
Murmuring, hissing,
Broken by gentle rain.

Over there,
Milky damask,
Stroking bare tops
With silken lover's touch,
Caressing cories,
Softening bold braes
Bathe in balmy air,
Laden with meadowsweet
Clinging to flared nostrils,
And deliquescing wrack rot.

Otters tunnel the shore,
To grip a limpet,
Infectious joy!

That shiny stone, moving water in a vee,
Is a seal's head.

If still, it's a rock.

Morven, Lochaber

Coming to Binsness

By pebbled tidal private
Sweep by Broom of Moy
Kincorth Clodymoss
Solo southern side
North from Forres'
Distant granite needles
Haven of hovering ospreys
Seeking whittling
On Culbin
Safe from shifting sands
Leeward Findhorn's quiet cove
Drynachen to Califer
Stretch of fir'd fields
Through trees, Findhorn
White and squat to take
Wester beatings hurricane gale and hail
(contd.)

Late summer's eve
Last of Sun's sweet balm
Five generations of Love
Reside in bricks and
Stone steading
Soft mossed grass yields
Beneath a tread
Joy of family feuding
Mohican mergansers
Saw billed to catch fry by
Generous Findhorn
In tide brown steel blue
Against the river's waves
Findhorn of
Distant crying seals
Across the wind
Siren sound on
Sand bar'd Firth
Yew Pine Beech
Arraviste Sycamore
Generous Findhorn
Generous laird
Such kindness flows
Pain stauncher
Mirth oasis
Single pheasant's haunt
Bow-wingèd herons
Gloaming croaking to roost

Binsness, Morayshire

Coming to Daless

Take the path by two ways -

From Dulsie, straight, then twisting,
Along broad Findhorn's soft sedged banks,
Before pinching turns of Banchor's gorges,
Marbled cattle,
Fat tailed sheep, Nordic fir.

Rise - fall
Along the river's course,
A quick sigh to take the view,
Shards of fear on a one-track precipice,
Each yard a step obscure,
Of adverse camber,
Incognito to oncoming,
Falling by Carnoch, easing hearts and hands
Tautened on the wheel, to Drynachen.

Or-

From Cawdor, past Cose,
Crossing curlews' cusp of moor and meadow,
Hen harrier's flight,
Peregrine's stoop.
Flat past knocks, braes and butts,
Blind summits, holding breath,
Around a bend
Along the steepness edge,
Broad based Douglas,
Binding banks to hold the slope,
Sighting flash up Findhorn's lavish valley,
Rich magnanimous flood plain,
To tree haloed Daless.

Then from Drynachen,
Bracken brushing, willowherb and whins,
Harum-scarum above thrashing, roiling spates,
Lifting high along cliff-pincered brink,
Held by gabions against slides,
Potholed, precipitous, steeply down glissading mamelon,
Fording the boundary burn.
Haven-heaven sanctuary.

Daless, Nairnshire

Curlew I

Out the North came full face slapping - sleet,
Too wet to counter Spring's urging,
Only vengeful swansong winter's wind on edge.

Gulls,
Chimney hustlers swooping,
Bickering with good reason,
Jostling for space along tiled ridges,
Balletic necks, looks of love
Bring little truce by raucous keening.

A recent waxèd tide in wane,
Now here is curlew.
Waiting, with stilted gait, patrolling,
Knowing when bladder wrack,
Mud and water bring her to
Command this familiar aromatic confluence.

Incongruous avian Numenius.
New Moon,
Describes your gentle crescent
Curve-beaked investigator
Of tidal boundaries dipping,
Searching for salty morsel
Crustacean feasts,
Fruit of life's sustenance down the soft foreshore.

Across the Bay on lofty ground,
Pressed by greys and steely,
Obscured high places,
Shining snow in sun-blessed breaks,
Slow-motion cloud fires' smoke,
Twist and lick from hearths of rock and ice,
Where moor and fallow meet,
Where Thane of late,
Cold these thirty years,
Has seen the wind erase
Father's footprints in the peat.

Here too, onomatopoeic curlew.

Your mournful trill, vibrato cry
Moves this man and mountains.
Over long-horizoned sand seas
And summer's upland leys
Stubble, fallow, grasshopper, beetle
Vacuumed, sealing my memories.

Who else has blue-grey legs and why?
Nesting in a scrape,
Scourged and scorched in your innocence
By ever present man,
To see, to hear last of your kind and song taken,
How lonely I shall be.

Findhorn, Morayshire

Curlew II

Curlew, I have found you
By Findhorn's widening river bend,
Stilted stepping fresh sheep bitten sward,
Sweet golden whins of Cailleach,
And sticky broom.

Your trilling - thrilling - fluting calls
Bounce off steepening braes,
Over alder, rowan, birch,
Dulled by early blushing heather,
Shaded under yet cold, barren places.

My heart jumps to see your scrape is here,
Tandem with oystercatchers' hueeping,
Hard by flourish daubs of lilac willowherb,
Fresh run salmon, grouse, roe.

Hidden in plain sight,
Veiled in cloaks of speckled bars and brown,
Eluding fox, weasel, eagle eyes,

In stillness.

In stillness,

Enthralled, I watch you call your young to flight,
Downy innocence.
You are real as just sawn wood.

Now I am here again in autumn's later days,
You have mastered mysteries of air and water,
Cobwebs dewed on the field's gate,
Last ospreys' chance of late-run fish.

Maybe you follow them to other summers.

While I...

All I see is the dent you made,
The easter wind now searching,
Turn my thoughts to nearing crunching frost.

Daless, Nairnshire

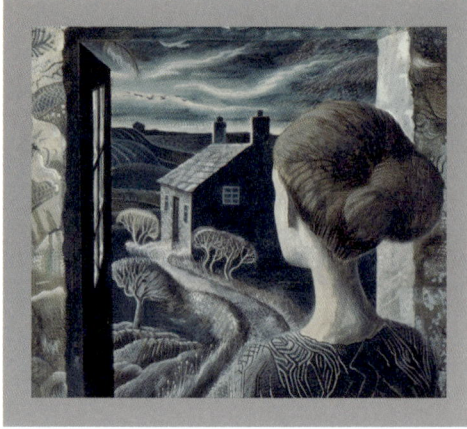

Euphemia Fogwatt's Lamentation

Snow begins at Lhanbryde
Quick and thick it lies,
Norther blasts clench the earth,
Spooking the ponies.
They kick and buck at one another.

I find Euphemia, her face set-to,
Gritted jaw and grimace,
Now thwarted she tells me,
From daily drudge and duties.

I see time falling
Heavy in her head,
Turning to a troubled and madding view,
Sitting as we are, by a just lit kitchen
Range softly crackling,
Smells of hot, sweet, black tea
Coming down generations,
Across cold stone flags.
We drink sherry.

Reminisce those innocent years of girlhood,
Singing hymns, though not for fun,
- only to be heard -
We saw how rich they were,
Laughed and cried our socks off,
Lasting 'til the over-morrow
Assuaged by rage and chocolate,
Rage and chocolate.

Our tears pour,
Keenly feeling razor's wound of what is lost,
When we and the other girls ran free in forests
Over years of fallen pine needles
Softening our path
Kissing our feet
While evening's intense stillness
Made a mirror on the loch.

Euphemia always knows when
Snows are coming.
What auburn leaves are left
Hang heavy in hedges,
Clacking in the wind.
Skeins from Canada and
Siberia arrive in
Thick chattering clouds,
Swirling onto stubbles,
And sheep still on the hill – forfend.

The reek of fishermen
Comes out of photographs on the wall
Remembering Grandmother's grinding work,
A tholing Silver Darling as she was,
Listening, lusting for the sooch o' the sea,
Futtle in hand.

Potatoes at least, at last
Are in the barn –
Stob by seed by chat by ware,
Mingling with sodden earth's petrichor.
(contd.)

Memories flood in,
Sinking her heart, much mauled,
Like a sailor's caul
Taken to the deep by cannon balls.

Snow falls in ever larger flakes,
Subduing, silent.
Even wind is numbed by weight
Of the storm delivered on time with
Something strange for a wedding gift.

Euphemia says she longs for the Bay in late,
Still, spring afternoons,
Watching the ossifrage hover against
A leaden and blue backdrop,
Folded, falling, talons forrard,
Curling flesh of finnick and spieling,
Querying in a quiet voice,
"Which of grouse or chicken
Is most preferred
In the bordellos of Nairn and Inverness?"

To ease the grating, rasping bonds,
Euphemia rises from a wicker chair,
Tries to spot the wind
By window running condensation,
Upon which drippings we make futile wagers.
Then to the door,
A wetted finger,
To seek soft gyrating eddies,
In ripples on
Greenhouse butts,
Pinches of grass for accuracy,
Thrown to white oblivion,
All to clear the deadening blanket,
In her head and on her misted garden,
To release a comforting
Steady meditation of normality.

Stifle, wither, frog, pastern,
Her soft hands recollecting reins
On mornings of condensing breath,
Feeling ponies' mouths
In snaffles, cantles, curb chains.

Smells of October sweeping from the Firth,
Looking towards short days of
Curry combs, straw bedding,
Her own close-coupled eye for horseflesh,
When last day of autumn
Becomes first day of winter.

Euphemia ever yearns
For long faded grandeur,
Monogrammed surcingles,
Melting into rushing,
White-spumed waves
Falling foaming on the beach,
A place of penance for her detested -
Those who love too much
The calling of lighted shop windows.

Seeing herself on the wings of crows on missions
Of vengeance, self-reproach,
Euphemia longs for her Light body to be cloaked,
Taken on myriad odysseys…

…in her mind,
When once a child in moonlight
Under ruined battlements
Smudged by staining verdigris,
Hearing running rigging slapping masts,
Stays' humming moans,
In boatyards or on the water,
Was heaven.

I had realised for many years
Euphemia ever took low roads,
Slow roads to satisfy diversions
Of derelict's glassless windows,
Through whose dark,
Mysterious maws came doves
Flapping from rafters, rusting gutters,
Bow roofed sheds
By tracks and lanes
Taking herself for fleeting moments
Out of the too small box of life
She made herself,

And think -
(contd.)

Think herself be drawn to a rich, pinking spring evening,
For her own spoonful of earth with whisky
Given to bairns by midwives.

From darksome glens of stupendous depths
In her head,
She tells me tales,
The wildest and most extravagant imaginable -
Cathedral's high vaulted naves,
Boundless caverns filling her mind's sky,
Another fitful night of toss and turn beckoning.

With this and more in her abstract shambles,
Warming by the fire,
Assailed by voices and woes from her inner deep,
Seduced by dreamworld's dramas,
Euphemia abruptly hears
"The living have the last word"
Takes a deep breath of sudden knowing,
Leaving me sleeping,
She heads for the drifts.

Banchor, Nairnshire

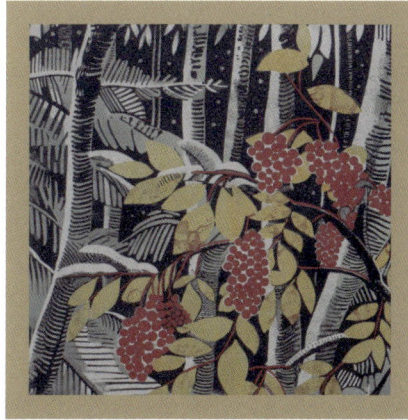

Moray September

Days of laze and summer haze are done
Faint intimations mark the end -

Mustard clusters on silver birches
Carmine bunches on rowans
Ash is bruised and bowed
Golden bracken broken
Vermilion cherries well in wane

Please take my fruit
Multi-seeded bramble
Please take my bounty that we live again
Our hips sloes haws
Are benison for you

Tawny hazel bistre
Leaves in crisping crunching umber
(contd.)

45

Stinking Willie
Culloden debacle's answer to
Bloody Butcher
Vulgaris by name and nature
Woeful plant
Bent in atrophy you fuscous poisoner

Russet tufts in the leys

Apple pear plum gean

The air has edge

Findhorn steadies for winter spates
When wind will grouch, bellyaching under doors
Rip squealing through gapped stone walls

Green to khaki sepia tints
Broom pods fit to burst

Burns, braes take your last drink of late summer air
My exhalation soon returns to mist again

Just here in this land
Is a moment free of man's hand

Daless, Nairnshire

Ploughing Match

DERV caught our throats one late autumn afternoon,
Happening on a ploughing match,
My would-be crofter girl in tow,
At Wester Greens in a stubble field,
A sea of Fordsons, Fergies,
And lubing Nuffields,
Weathered men with weathered hands,
Spanners tinkle-tankling,
Hanging off the ploughs.

We lunched on griddle cakes and turkey soup.
Talked of fuel, of crude, of feed and food and
All the changes, all the countless changes.

"I never desired conformity in my fruit.
Uniformity of apples has me baffled"
Dreamer Farmer opined.
"I like my strawberries with bumps"
Swilling more broth,
"To take away the tractor breath" he said.

David Brown lover, King of Quines,
Pouring tea from a flask into bone China offered,
"They own the bellies of the people,
They have us by the guts they do"
"Who is they?" requested crofter girl.
Griddle maker Queen of Quines laughing, chimed:
"Why, the self-proclaimed custodians of the land of course!"
(contd.)

Dreamer Farmer, drooling at a working vintage thresher:
"All is palm oil sodden, just for fun and profit.
Nutrition is an armoury of foods martial,
Yes, martial would be right,
Materiel for Nature's end.
Defcon - sterilise our souls with woebegone weed be gone.
Brigade, Assail, Ambush, Black Hawk and Capture
Shall and do counter nematodes,
With extreme prejudice.
Deadline, pernicious bait for slugs and snails, Nature's larders.
Reaper, Requiem and Respect, toxic to bees for three hours only mind,
While Tombstone and Venom kill all sucking insects,
Yes, all of them."

Against these raucous blasts of science and satellite,
Seeking memory, we are water, earth, air, fire
Each of us dissembled,
Lost in thoughts of our own makings and doings.

Lossiemouth, Morayshire

48

Pluscarden To Lethan

Along slopes, ranks of firs move
As my mother's tresses in the wind,
Ripple-flash their under needles silver.
Sycamores bend to the rush,
Exulting, clearing air through their boughs.

And roar,
'Are you listening?'

This is the haunt of hawk and roe,
Where Little People roam
Hidden by thorn and thicket,
Living by bramble and yew.

I a traveler,
Am drawn by mossy nosegays of
Gentle autumn rot,
Roots, sedges, boggy edges,
Leaves whirlygigging, widdershins
As wilded children in a playground,
Hastening hither thither,
Rushing down the wind.
Hastening to humus, worms,
Spores of fruiting fungus.
(contd.)

Sonsy rain drops bounce the road,
Hissing in the trees.
Brushed slate and battleship,
Seeks the rising way to meet the sky.

Made for passing moments of reflection,
A pull-in
Where collide Man and Nature.
So convenient for microwave and wrapper,
Bottles, bones and builders' taplash
And while about it,
Bags of ullage and atrophy
To see out ten thousand years of drip drip hereto.

By the road, hapless hopeless wire
To snag a stoat,
Scratch a fox,
Rip a badger,
Ligature on cambium.

A toothless wandering man came by and asked the time.
He did.

At last, the height of Lethan.
Fold upon fold upon fold of distance,
Roll back in smoky mists across the Firth.
In forest edge, tree-tops dance with rippling sward,
Freedom in their gale's ecstasy.

Findhorn, Morayshire

The Arrival

Bresse Gaulois arrived in yestereven's gloaming
Boxed in his full pomp and trumpet
Into the expectant henhouse with
Blue legs white feathers red comb

Blew in with faintest softly breath of
New spring grass before Lambing Snows
Under the burn and
Last year's beech leaves
Still rattling in the hedge

Ard-Daraich, Ardnamurchan (50 words)

The Herdsman

For Jude

The Herdsman, lonely as the Moon at sun-sight,
Trudges upward to his distant flock,
His vulpine cur to foot,
Beside deep mossed dry-stone walls
Striding the hills league upon league,
Noting as always, in awe,
The tireless muscle
And rough worn hands that
Wrought such testaments to survival.

Low-lying, late Autumn's mists
Enthral stands of nearby pines,
Splitting glaucous braes where once was moor.
Here last of summer's swallows have taken fill,
Drinking from sacred springs
Known only to them,
To Him, the cur, his vagrant flock
And the once gemmed-wingèd moth,
Dulled and dying
In this pellucid dawn.

He walks between two worlds,
Where copse and single trees leant eastward,
Bent at will by the wind.
The walls are wet,
The wind warm yet,
And willowherb still colour drenched
As other banks and verges gone to seed.

He finds no use for wealth and baublery.
He laughs at their richness,
Clinging as they must to outward expressions,
Judging others by a dimming light in their own souls.
He is drawn rather to inner manifestations -
Voices of streams and rills,
A river's constant, complex viola's note,
Cries of the night plover,
Hidden coverlets of tussock,
A lek,
A snapped twig,
A coloured stone,
A rose bush in lavish disarray,
To die on the road under a hedge,
Air His free inheritance.

Now long days are ousted,
The Herdsman again can brood and chafe
Against the dark bulk of beliefs,
Remembering always to have kindling in the footwell,
Eschewing the dreary sport of killing time,
Waiting for faded lustres of the chase.
(contd.)

Leaving behind the calm crossing's caressing waters,
My prow crunches on shingle
Hissing and rattling with each retreating wave.
I too am drawn by the night plover's call,
Her voice of ringing silver –
'How worthy of reverence is the Ocean'
She declares in a mother-of-pearl shell against my ear,
Seducing my eyes to the hills where
Herdsman and cur
Stride ever onward.

Daylight washes over me as the tide,
As my own life shall at the last.
I see the Hoofmark Men's shadows
Track droves
And moors
For spoors
Of the rustled,
Knowing each beast by individual print.

Out of driftwood and tangle,
Winter spates will certain wash away,
Will bring news
To the foreshore of these higher places,
Whither I am called
To be wrapped in long snows.

I set out, sure of mien,
To the uplands.

The constant Herdsman, cur and I will face,
Full frosted,
Devoid of a moment's shelter from Truth,
Memories of perfect, ceaseless service as
'Adam once walked in clear-eyed innocence, in Paradise,
To talk with the Lord in the cool of the Day'
On ice breathed ground,
In starlit veils of children's tears,
The welcome dark of night.

He and I are shy lovers of leys,
Swales, flowered meadows,
Lapped in manifold silence.
We never come to want,
We thank God for the Brotherhood of the Poor,
We stand on the battlefield of the World
Square to the foe,
For the World has been stripped of Her bright colours,
Standing naked, nary a stitch,
Waiting for the Coloured Robe to clothe Her tired stains.
Showing a pale, furrowed face
Under veins of lilac clouds,
She murmurs soft farewells and
Long forgotten Songs of the Scythe.

Banchor, Nairnshire

LET US DRINK HIBISCUS

At Doña Agustina's

Demise of a way of being
Brought me here
- Drinking fresh mint tea at nightfall -
Away with quarrel, dissonance,
- Lighting a fire -
With mouthfuls of dust
- Rolling a fag –
Watching the three
- Relinquished from control -
One, twirling her hair
- To find a warrior's nature -
Two, fingering taps of lassitude on the table
- Yielding to greater clarity -
Three, gazing, in silence to a hidden distance
- Soaking sops in leftover mole -
While we watched thunder stride
Across the mountains' faces.
A chihuahua on tip claw begged for rice,
Which was given

Amatlan, Morelos

59

Grandfather Tatawarri[1]

Grandfather, of course you know our minds,
We are one mind.

Grandfather, of course you know our hearts,
We are one heart.

For our hearts are rich and ready
To be in service,
To honour Creation
That we may pour in constant flow,

Compassion,

Love upon all,

Everlasting
Perpetual
Complete

Amatlan, Morelos (50 words)

---

[1] *The Fire in Wixaritari tradition, takings prayers and offerings to the ancestors*

Harris Hawk

"For melding of heartbeats and stability"
He said,
Holding the hawk close to his chest.
Hunting the old way,
Raptor gripping the left,
Reins in the right,
High in the stirrups
Guiding by thigh and calf,
Three in concert
Fashioned from countless arduous hours.

He has a look of the Steppes about him,
High cheekbones, eyes narrowed by sun,
Frown lines and crow's feet
From constant seeking glare.
Hunter and hawk scan,
Riding rough high ground,
Perhaps for hours
'til a rare chance comes.
(contd.)

Neaga, as she is first,
Young, needy, inexperienced,
Becomes a Prima,
When in full bloom.
Perched and hooded,
On her stand by the fire
In all-night vigil.

Dawn comes with early songs and
Chirrups from nearby trees,
Vultures catch earliest updraughts
Soaring off clifftops
In daily commute to municipal dumps,
Without fail.
Someone mentions nonchalantly
Their flesh is iridescent green.

The hunter places meat in circle of thumb and forefinger-
Food for Humari, Messenger of the Sun.
He removes her rufter,
She ruffles her feathers, morning stretch,
Eating fast, she tears for fear of robbers.

Hawk and hunter pet and mutter with one another,
She, seeking reassurance.
"Affection forms the tightest bond
For as long as we both shall live"
He said.

Amatlan, Morelos

62

Jalisco Sierras

We came in the month of flowers,
Tiny emerald frogs,
Biting winds, cold, cold rain.
Our medicines are coffee, honey, laughter,
Blue corn tortillas, hard salty fresh cheese,
Listening to the soft crackle of
Unwrapping boiled sweets
For the wee ones,
Under a smoke-trapping tarpaulin
Close around the fire.

Flowers drape slopes and
Valleys by roads
Reaching far horizons,
Dancing in breeze's thoroughfares,
Sodden by rains, parched by sun.
Around we sense
Monumental, elemental masses burgeoning,
In rock, firmament and forest.

I watch hands in offerings,
Long, slender fingers pointing to directions,
Others small, soft clasping intensity,
Holding wads of tobacco and copal,
Brief interlude before winter sets,
In the high Jalisco Sierras.
(contd.)

Clouds obscure the moon,
Dark, gelid,
We are lost in an enveloping cloak with
Spirit walkers, phantasms,
Long gone bears.

A night to astonish,
So vast it is.
Without fear in our diminution,
Possessed instead by surreal exhilarations,
For we are within Creation's days
With Light called into being.

Rain is coming.
The sheeting roof will bend and sink,
Rivulets will reach our feet,
Washing dust of yesterday away
This place of wolf and deer.

Fire smokes and crackles,
Our eyes run 'til sun sight
When cows cry for fodder,
Piglets, chicks and chickens around our feet,
Pine boles set afire in dawn's first blazing,
Sights to wax and wane my heart,
Cobwebs glistening on a five-bar gate,
Children stir and mewl.

We are naught but transient children of Nature,
Around Tatawarri[1] whose sparks are insight,
Gold and cobalt through the darkness,
Hungry for our offerings.

For a moment it is bitter cold,
We wait for promised things,
For in this age of machines,
We must be gentle mechanics,
For here are
Truth, Beauty and Love at their most raw.

Huejuquilla, Jalisco

M

When the Ocean spoke – twice,
I saw that She is Life
And Life is Love,
So, as you came up the sand,
Water falling from your body
Rippling and reflecting,
Your face of smiling sunshine,
I knew you know how to be touched
And let Her everlasting generosity
Move you

San Agustinillo, Oaxaca (50 words)

Masakatewarri[1]

What of Aire
The transparent one,
Showing yourself in rippling waters,
Quivering leaves, bending boughs?

You lift wings of
Soaring birds, butterflies, bees and beetles.

Oceans rage and spin, frothing at your touch
In cleansing destruction.
Leaves run down your hiding river flow
For you are Light Water,
Seed carrier.

Take prayers and orisons,
Our service and offerings
To ears of Ancestors that they
Hear our pleas.

---

[1] *Masakatewarri, Wixaritari Boy of the Wind*

You are settled fog,
Chariot of clouds,
Muffled thrum of a moth's flight,
Whispering feather tips of eagle's wings.

Trees susurrate your song.

By you, all things of Earth rise and fall.

Abuelo is moved by you and moves you.
Madre is kissed by you and kisses you.
Wimarri[2], mi hermana azul, is carried by you
Swirling, drifting, she falls through you.

Lightning splits to fall upon yourself in thunder.
You are calm morning zephyrs on my cheek.

On a nearby table, a single candle
Flickers in your night's soft shifts,
Raising overhead a passing firefly,
Fleeting star among stars,
Full of her dreams for tomorrow,
All the while in your thrall.

Poza de Quetzalcoatl, Morelos

---

[2] *Wimarri, Wixaritari Blue Girl of the Rain*

Mexpedition to Wixaritari's Wirikuta

Does the road ever end, cactus, mesquite,
Meandering ever upward,
Rocks ringing in midday heat?

We dance away a passing woe
Binding our hearts,
From strangers to lovers,
Engine clinging to thinning air
Where wandering goats take precedence,
Towards long awaited, sacred garden,
Wirikuta.

Past jagged horizons,
Take one step from the road
To wonder how those before us went here,
Scorpion, snake, spider, toad,
Vultures skirling thermal shimmered summits
To lift beneath beatless wings,
Pinprick eyes in search for dead or dying.

Hours pass, dissolving in a moment –

Wirikuta reaches out before us,
Haze softening early evening's outlines,
Earth writing her songs as clouds,
Their glancing shadows stroke distant slopes,
Quieting this landscape's ancient strength of life,
Driving awe deep within,
Formed by earthly forge and
Land slipped cliff faces.
I capture,
Etch this passing day in constant memory.

Green, flat, sierra bound, folds of dust
Where once Whale swam in innocence,
We take smaller roads by dry rock-strewn gulches,
Bumping potholed,
We pass a gentle beauty's tight black plait beside
Small, cultivated squares for iku[1]– life's very Mother centre.

---

[1]*Corn*

Dappled by evening's later workings,
Desert palms sentinel around us,
Cacti protect their precious water
With vicious thorn.

Paltemai's[2] long promised hallowed plateau,
At last,
Belovèd Wirikuta
Aureate as evening draws.
We seek hidden treasure upon
Sacred Tierra 'neath sacred Firmament,
River of Light[3], her darksome and stupendous chasm,
Derachen, Yikaisdaha, 'That which awaits dawn'.
Benefaction sought under pewtered milk sky
Of star pricked heron grey.

May thoughts of our hearts be words from our lips
By Grandfather Tatawarri's[4] constant Love,
Watching women in Mystery's most deep embrace,
To feel,
To hear wind soughing its low note
Through ocotillo's[5] tearing arms,
Visions of the Blue Deer, Corn, Eagle
And jikuri[6],
To be moved,
To have no thought of
'What time is the morning?'
To be free of tomorrow,
To be here.

San Luis de Potosi, Mexico

---

[2] *Maracate, Wixarika senior medicine man, Don Julian Candelario Carillo*
[3] *The Milky Way*
[4] *The Fire in Wixaritari tradition, taking prayers and offerings to the ancestors*
[5] *Type of cactus with long, thin leafy arms hiding a thick array of thorns*
[6] *Peyote*

Neikame

Neikame,
Beyond reach of los Puntos Elementos
Neikame
The trice a corn seed splits to sprout
Neikame,
Who cannot be refused.

From no constellation, one of twins,
A rock, wandering frozen outermost places
Until summoned.

Attending –
Overflowing in constant torrents of
Love, compassion to all beings, animate and inanimate
In this world, throughout the Cosmos.

My sister Wimarri, Blue Girl of the Rain
Her legs and arms around my chest and neck,
In tight embrace, tears soaking my hair,
Suffers greatly from our ways,

My brother, Masakatewarri, Boy of the Wind
Stained, fouled by foolishness,
Choking, he carries burdens of our prayer
To ears of Ancestors listening keenly for our song.

El Origen, Haramarra, Harayuavme,
Whence comes pure antediluvian service,
Offerings of simplicity for all to comprehend,
Without gods, to Creation herself, Mother of the Earth.
Abuela, sees her daughter made wretched.
She is forgotten,
Without whom we are nothing.

Tao, Grandfather,
Whose heart chakras in the palms of his hands
Pour forth in perpetual flow – abundance,
Is agonised by greed.

Tobacco, copal, cacao, amaranth and honey,
Imbue our hearts' desire for grace, wisdom.
Through Tatawarri[1], offer, con permiso,
To los Kakauyarris, los Puntos Elementos,
Las Estés de la Luz, Ángeles, Guías,
Guardianes de las Alturas, Cuauhtémoc, Kayumari,
This fleeting handful for
Their eternal promise of harmony.

Amatlan, Morelos

---

[1] *The Fire in Wixaritari tradition, takings prayers and offerings to the ancestors*

71

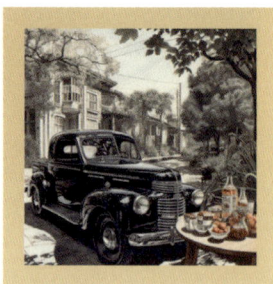

Passing Time In Amatlan

Let us drink hibiscus.
In cool air
Of early winter's still warming sun,
Smoothed rocks to sit upon,
Walls awash with bougainvillaea,
Smells of tortillas cooking on hot-plates
Fresh dropped dung
From nomad cows and horses.

So, we drank hibiscus,
Rich, red with sodden petals,
Poured by la señorita with a silver tooth.

Lovers wander on the cobbles.

Bigger than a girl's hand,
Josephinas[1],
Whiter than royal hempen cloth -
Glide,
Their time near done,
Among long flags of drying clothes,
Over roofs,
Above laurel shaded streets,
Where to pass midday's torpor
Watching overladen pick-ups,
Smoking, groaning with plenty,
Come to the peaceful market by the road.

Amatlan, Morelos

---

[1] *Ganyra Josephina, giant white butterfly*

S I

Silhouetted in the mountains' setting sun
Fervent as a namaste to Mother,
You stirred me with your utter depth
Such that I heard your heart's call
Whisper a sweet softness
Into the void
Where all is known
And heard.
An answer came - in silence -
Be as you already are.

Acapulco, Guerrero (50 words)

S II

You have a smile to light the dark
Clarity as bells' peal to service
Wisdom beyond your years

Lips to kiss - constantly
Your body made to wrap in my arms
Iris open that I may dive your Soul
Unhindered innermost
In gratitude for letting me be
Letting me be

Tepoztlan, Morelos (50 words)

S III

As you are present in my mind,
(I am far away)
We are atop these belovèd rocks
Puffed and flushed
By our exertions
To gain this high place
Thus, we may feel

- Together –

How Abuelo and Abuela
Can and do overwhelm us
With Love and Compassion.

This is my prayer.

Amatlan, Morelos (50 words)

Unrequited

You want me gently to run the back of
My hand over your softness,
You know it will assuage
Raging hurt.

Melancholy of your eyes
Brings understanding.

Your strength constrained by hidden chains.
Disparaged.
Your beauty pushed aside –

Wondering how it came to this.

I am no knight in shining armour,
But by Jove I desire to embrace your whole,
Caress your woes farewell,
Clasp you tight in new adventures,
Through loss, joy and intemperance.

Shall we step into new lives,
Firmly side by side,
Call you mine,
In Truth, in Love?

In Love.

When I gently run the back of
My hand over your softness,
You shall have been comforted.

Amatlan, Morelos 01/22

NAPIER MARTEN

Napier has felt a deep connection with the natural world since boyhood.
An inveterate traveller, he is drawn to wild and less trodden parts of the globe.
Varied locations speak through his poetry. From an early age he saw there is a
wisdom beyond rational human constructs of conditioned experience.
This evolved during his upbringing on his family's estate in South West England
where interest in ecology, the environment and life's cycles became the basis for
his poetry which frequently alludes to the importance of reconnection to Nature.

Napier has set up charitable foundations whose aims are to support First Nations
around the world, focusing on understanding and sharing the need for global
recognition of our ancient and profound relationship with cetaceans.

Napier has had a varied career including rural management, arborist, hedge-layer,
actor, helicopter pilot, and aviation and arboricultural consultancy. He is an
active cranio-sacral practitioner and has a small farm dedicated to local
flora and fauna.